My 9/11—Through In-Flight Eyes

By
Terry Horniacek

Published by BOBM Publishing, LLC

2021

MY 9/II

Through inflight eyes

TERRY HORNIACEK

ISBN 978-0-578-99160-3
First Printing: 2021
USA
Ordering Information:

Quantity sales. On quantity purchases by corporations, associations, and others—orders by trade bookstores and wholesalers, contact BOBM Publishing, LLC at info@businessofbooksmastermind.com

DEDICATION

This book is dedicated to the passengers and families of United Flight 93 and their crew: Jason Dahl, LeRoy Homer, Sandy Bradshaw, CeeCee Lyles, Wanda Green, Debbie Welsh, and Lorraine Bay.

My mother, Kathy Petrasek Mcgowan, held my hand through this difficult journey I am about to share. She taught me that I have a God to lean on through my afflictions and addictions in this life. She was a role model and my hero. I love you, Mom.

Anne Leeser Brown is a beautiful woman and has been a second mother to me throughout my life. She often was my shoulder to cry on as I walked through this trauma of 9/11. She was my mother's best friend and always a strong, positive person in my life. I love you, Anne.

TABLE OF CONTENTS

ACKNOWLEDGMENTS

Acknowledgements: I would like to extend my heartfelt appreciation to my family for their constant support. To my children, Kristen, Katie, Donnie, and Jason and Jason's wife, Leanne, thank you for believing in me and supporting me on this journey. Thanks to my brother, Steve, for always being my best friend and confidant. To my aunts Linda and Laurie, thank you for my spiritual guidance; the prayers and love have inspired me to achieve success. A special thanks to Don for always loving and taking care of our children. Finally, thank you to my friends Melanie and Jennifer for the hope you give me through your experiences and friendship.

PRELUDE

My 9/11—Through In-Flight Eyes will give you insight into the September 11, 2001, terrorist attacks from the flight attendants' and the United Airlines employees' horrific experiences. This book will walk you through the dark side of the human psyche as it emotionally crumbles from trauma and grief. I will also share the faith that I had and how I've learned to trust that faith as I fought through the misdiagnosis of bipolar disorder and the challenges of physical abuse, mental hospitals, and drug addiction. I will share my journey through acceptance, strength, healing, and ultimate survival as I fight through these trials and trauma.

PART I: THE
SHOCKWAVE

2001 AWARD

I was doing well—better than well—before it all happened. In September 1999, I found myself as an in-flight-services coordinator for United Airlines in Newark, New Jersey. My job requirements included ensuring compliance with federal air regulations by having the correct number of crew members on each aircraft and checking in all flight attendants before each flight. Also, I would brief the crews, which involved giving them passenger manifests and preparing them for departure. I worked closely with the crew desk in Chicago, constantly reviewing the crew assignments for the flights. I felt so fulfilled at my position there. To tell you the truth, I never planned on leaving.

I excelled at my job quickly, and I loved it. The flight attendants treated me with such love and kindness. I looked forward to going to work each day. I began to take on extra tasks in the office, such as updating training manuals and informational manuals.

In early 2001, I worked hard to organize our first health fair in the airport. It began as an idea for the employees to do a blood drive. Then it turned into a full health fair for the airport and its employees. It included blood donations, blood-pressure checks, eye checks, testing for different viruses, heart and blood-sugar testing, and mammograms. As I contacted different professionals about the event, I found them all willing to donate their time to such a worthy cause. So, United Airlines' health fair became a large success. I received a lot of praise for the efforts I had put into it.

At the end of March, my manager notified me that I had been nominated for a corporate and a divisional award for humanitarian of the year because of my involvement in the fair. I was floored at the prospect of being recognized for my work from a corporate level, all the way from United headquarters in Chicago.

Ultimately, I won two awards: the divisional and the regional humanitarian awards. What an honor it was. I was invited to two different events in Chicago to be honored with the bigwigs of the company. I treasure the crystal awards that I received. United wined and dined the award recipients for an entire weekend and praised the achievements that had brought us to this function. I spent some time with our board of directors and the chief executive officer of the company, Jim Goodwin, as he congratulated each candidate.

It was an enjoyable time and a proud moment for me. These events only made me want to press harder every day at doing better as in-flight-services coordinator.

CHAPTER ONE

September 11, 2001, started as Tuesday morning on which I had expected to be off work. I received a call at 4:30 a.m. to cover the desk as an in-flight-services coordinator. Rob Perillo, my supervisor, said that our coordinator for the day had called out sick, so I went in to cover.

Sometime after 9/11, a flight attendant named April mentioned to me that the Muslim men had not prayed in the baggage claim that morning. That seems important now, because every morning, my colleagues and I saw them there as we came into work. Barefoot and on their knees, these men would face the sunrise and pray. Every day, this happened—except for September 11. Did these men know of the plan that day, or were they our hijackers? That thought constantly comes to my mind. Did anyone else happen to notice that, I wonder?

That day, I opened the office at Newark Airport at four forty-five a.m. The first crew then checked in at five for a six o'clock flight to Chicago. The crews for another six o'clock departure and a seven o'clock departure also checked in at this point.

A routine morning involved the crews' arriving approximately one hour before their flights. After checking in, they would pull up their passenger lists and do a flight briefing. Then they would socialize a little and check their mailboxes. They would head to their gates forty-five minutes before departure and begin boarding passengers fifteen minutes later.

The office was usually filled with flight attendants coming and going. They and I often had some great conversation and a few laughs before they left for the gates.

At seven o'clock, the flight attendants with eight o'clock departures checked in. One of the crews checking in at this time was the Flight 93 crew, who had a flight to San Francisco that day. As the five flight attendants came in one by one, I distinctly remember the time I had with each of them.

Flight attendant Sandy Bradshaw appeared first. She always arrived early because she commuted to Newark and stayed at a downtown crash pad overnight before her flights. She was pleasant as usual, beaming. She signed in for her flight and proceeded to the computer room to pull up her paperwork.

Before Sandy and other flight attendants left for the gates, she pulled out a picture of her new little girl, Alex. We all looked at the photo. Sandy looked so proud as her face shone with joy. She talked about possibly going on leave to stay home with that new baby. We were all excited for Sandy to take the time off to be a mom to Alex.

Flight attendant Lorraine Bay came into the office next. Everyone would describe Lorraine the same way: sweet, quiet, and full of love for everyone. She was a kind woman and always showed compassion and interest in everyone else. She spread her love with a pleasant hello to all of us, spreading compliments as usual and making us feel great.

When Lorraine came to the desk to sign in, she read the notices posted on the counter. One was an update on a sick coworker of ours, Pam. Lorraine wrote down Pam's address and went into the computer room to join the others. When Lorraine came out for her preflight briefing, she filled out a get-well card for Pam and mailed it from the gate that morning before boarding the flight. Pam received that bittersweet card on Friday, September 14, 2001.

CeeCee Lyles was a reserve flight attendant. Reserve status means you work when needed, so you must be available within four hours to work a trip. You also have to be available for work on your reserve days. CeeCee commuted from Florida to Newark, so she also stayed at a crash pad. She did not want to fly that day because she was on her last day of reserve and hoped to fly back to Florida a day early. This wonderful mother had five children and her husband waiting for her.

However, we needed CeeCee for the flight to San Francisco that day. She never complained about it. She just smiled and signed in, but I could sense her disappointment. CeeCee was the most junior flight attendant on the crew for Flight 93. She had only been flying since fall 2000.

Flight attendant Debbie Welsh came rushing in at the last minute. It shocked me to see her name on the crew list because she always worked nights. Debbie said she'd traded shifts with another flight attendant so she could attend a few auditions with her actor husband, Patrick.

Unlike most flight attendants, Debbie wore her hat with her uniform. Debbie was full of class. She had flown for many years with Eastern and Kiwi Airlines before United. Debbie had an aura about her that was full of life. She stood about six feet tall and was like sunlight when she smiled.

Debbie also came behind my desk and gave me a big hug to tell me that she was clear of the melanoma she had been battling. We shared a moment of tears before she scurried off to print her paperwork. Debbie would be the purser on this trip, meaning she would be the head flight attendant and work in first class.

Last but not least was flight attendant Wanda Green. She also came running in late, not feeling so well. I sent the rest of the crew to the gates as Wanda decided whether she needed a replacement. She was complaining of heart palpitations. Concerned, I told her that I could use our standby flight attendant that morning instead. Much like a reserve flight attendant, a standby comes in and sits for four hours in case she or he needs to work a flight.

On the day of 9/11, the standby flight attendant I would have used was Evelyn "Evy" Wagner. She had her luggage ready to go and was quite willing to work the San Francisco trip. But Wanda decided to work the trip and see a doctor when she returned to Newark. I sent her to the gate about twenty minutes late.

Evy came to me a month or two later, and we shared a cry. She could have been on that fateful flight. I believe Evy has something wonderful to do in this world. Something—fate, luck, destiny— spared her life. Do any of us understand?

Of the flights hijacked on 9/11, only Flight 93 left the gate late. Their delay lasted approximately twenty-two minutes. I believe those twenty-two minutes gave the passengers and crew the chance to try to take the plane back from the hijackers. Still, our girls (as I affectionately refer to all United flight attendants) would end their trip as unwilling participants on a mission of pure malice and destruction.

The Stonycreek Township, located in Somerset County, Pennsylvania, would be the resting place of our crew and passengers of Flight 93, who became our first line of defense in the war on terrorism. Lorraine Bay, Sandy Bradshaw, Debbie Welsh, CeeCee Lyles, and Wanda Green—these women spent their last moments on the ground with the in-flight office staff at Newark Airport. I will always remember the conversations and the time spent with these women. I am proud to have known them and cherish those moments spent with them before that horrific morning flight.

The cockpit crew was Captain Jason Dahl and First Officer LeRoy Homer. LeRoy was a junior pilot with the company. Authorities believe they died early in the flight, but no doubt they were true heroes who desperately tried to keep control of their aircraft.

OFFICE STAFF

The only staff in the office first thing in the morning were Eileen, the morning supervisor who came in at six a.m.; Linda MacDonald, an administrative secretary; Sallie, another administrative secretary; Mary, the administrative coordinator; and, of course, me. This small team was a typical size for this point in the morning.

NOTIFY MANAGEMENT

Shortly after 8:45 a.m., a flight attendant rushed to my desk with a panicked look on her face, an expression of horror.

She said, "A plane just hit the Empire State Building."

She had seen this on television in the crew lounge and shook as she tried to tell me. I did not register what I was hearing. She repeated, "*A plane just hit the Empire State Building!*"

I left my desk and ran next door to see the news for myself. (As it turned out, the flight attendant had mistaken preliminary information about what had just transpired.) I couldn't believe what I saw. Praying that the crashed plane wasn't a United flight, I ran to inform our domicile manager, Linda Duffey.

Most would describe Linda as a professional and calm person. As I told her of the events at the World Trade Center, she instructed me to contact our headquarters in Chicago to see if they had any information on which aircraft had crashed. She also got on the phone to contact her boss, Diane.

When I attempted to call Chicago, I realized that our phones were down. The only contact we had was through ACARS, or the Aircraft Communications, Addressing, and Reporting System. This digital datalink system can transmit short messages between aircraft and ground stations using airband radio or satellite. However, this system couldn't give us the kind of communications link we needed at that time.

Despite this setback, I knew I had to keep trying to contact Randy, who was our in-flight scheduler in Chicago for the day. His job was to fill the empty crew slots for understaffed planes. Often the coordinator (in this case, me) calls in with available crews, and the scheduler puts them on the trip. That day, I had already called Randy and asked him to add CeeCee Lyles and Sandy Bradshaw. Randy had okayed the crew list and added their names.

Eventually, my call got through to Chicago. When I informed Randy of the crash, he said he thought it was a flight from American Airlines or one of their commuter-airline partners, Midway. I am ashamed to admit it, but I felt instant relief when I heard American and not United. After all, I had sent several flights out already that morning, flights with my friends on them. Somehow it would be easier if nobody knew the people who had crashed. Randy and I agreed to keep each other updated with information as we received it.

During the attacks, much of the action happened just outside the airport, across the Hudson River. We could see black clouds of smoke in the air.

The flight attendants in the office at this point had run next door to the lounge, which had a TV, to see what was going on. I also went back to the television after contacting Chicago. I had not been in the lounge for two minutes when the next plane hit. Not just *a* plane— one of *our* planes. The United Airlines logo was quite distinct as the second aircraft hit the South Tower and people jumped from the burning buildings.

Some flight attendants screamed; others were crying, and a couple just stood there in shock, as I did. Whatever else we did at that moment, we all held onto each other in that lounge.

For a moment, I forgot I was at work and in charge of the in-flight-services desk. I ran back to the office to notify management of the second crash. Had that United plane carried one of the crews that I had met with and sent to the gates for departure that morning?

SHOCK

I vividly remember the feeling that came over me. I immediately felt fear, a sense of worry that I don't ever recall feeling before. I felt my heart racing and felt as if I couldn't catch my breath. My body seemed to go limp. I felt my knees giving out; I began to feel very light-headed. I was ready to drop; I was completely weak.

I realized later that what I was feeling was anxiety. It was so overpowering that I had to sit and breathe into a bag. I managed to get through that feeling, which lasted a few short minutes. Although it continued to surface, usually followed by tears, I was able to work my way through it. Linda Staffieiri, one of the supervisors, talked me through these tense moments.

CALLS BEGIN

Calls began coming into our office by the second when the second plane hit the tower, but we could not make outgoing calls. Family members and flight attendants called in, keeping us informed during that short time right after the crashes.

The flight attendants who were with me in the office were distraught. Jeanne, Ellen, and April had arrived early and were waiting to check in for their flights. When the phones went dead, Ellen began to panic, saying that the airports might be targets for attack. The thought had never crossed my mind until I heard that. Now I was really scared.

In 2001, around 45 percent of all Americans had use of a personal cell phone.[1] I was not one of them. Jeanne offered to call my family on her cell phone to let them know I was okay, but she had no outgoing phone service. I gave her the phone numbers as we all hugged. She promised to call when she had service outside the airport.

The events seemed to unfold so quickly. The chaos of the phones ringing made the tension and anxiety extreme. I felt as if I were in a total state of confusion or loss of control of the situation for a bit. Several times, I had to walk away from the ringing telephones and take a few deep breaths to calm down. On one hand, I felt I could handle the unknown task we were facing. On the other,

---

[1] "Number of Mobile Wireless Connections per 100 People in the United States from 2001 to 2011," Mobile Wireless Penetration Rate in the US 2001–2011, Statista, accessed August 14, 2021, https://www.statista.com/statistics/184946/estimated-mobile-wireless-penetration-rate-in-the-us-since-2001-nruf/

I felt myself getting worked up, crying and talking fast—almost like having a panic attack.

STAFF ARRIVES

By now, the supervisors had reached the office, and it was after nine o'clock. Thomas, who worked in customer service, had arrived and began training at the desk with me to answer the phones.

In happier circumstances, we all looked forward to working with Thomas. He was a hysterical combination of charm and charisma. Always happy, he spread that joy around the room. He seemed to live by the motto, "Like me or not, this is who I am."

I believe Thomas replaced me after I left work in 2002. I am glad he was there on September 11; I will not forget the strength he brought to me.

LOCATING ALL CREWS

Let's face it. If you were watching the attacks happen that morning, this obviously was not an accident. To watch two planes crash into the Towers—anyone with an ounce of sense would realize that. Unfortunately, you lose all your sense at a moment so horrifying as that, and you aren't quite in touch with what you are seeing. What my thoughts were at the time, and I remember them as vividly as if it were yesterday—I felt so shaken and confused while trying to locate everyone and trying to come up with an answer as to why these planes had just hit. What possible explanation could there be?

Then I began to worry about the flights which had left earlier. Where was each flight that had taken off from the United Newark gates? I began pulling up flights on the computer, one after another. Normally, if you pull up a flight on the computer, you get the list of flight attendants, the destination, and the departure and arrival times. As I pulled up flight numbers, everything seemed okay for the moment. Each flight listed its crew, so I assumed everything was okay with United.

I continued the process until finally American Airlines Flight 11 out of Boston showed "Records Secure," and that told me something was wrong with that flight. This alternate message was a real warning to me.

FIRST HIJACKING CALL

Around 9:30 a.m., Thomas answered the first call from Phil Bradshaw, husband of flight attendant Sandy Bradshaw. Phil said calmly that Sandy had phoned from Flight 93. Four men wearing red bandanas and wielding box cutters had hijacked the plane. Phil's call was the first we knew of Flight 93's involvement in the attacks.

Phil was clearly shocked by Sandy's call. He said he did not know what to say to her on the phone and seemed distraught over that fact alone. He said he would phone back if he heard anything else.

RANDY IN SCHEDULING

We didn't have much time to process Phil's call. Randy, our in-flight scheduler in Chicago, soon called back and confirmed that some of our flights were missing. He wasn't sure exactly which ones at this point, but the thought of it terrified me. I continued pulling up flight after flight on my desktop computer, trying to locate each one. Were they on the ground or out there somewhere? It was the most frightening experience of my life.

I could feel the pain and tension in the back of my neck going right up the back of my head. I guess it was stress, anxiety, and tension. That pain stayed with me the rest of the day.

The flight attendants, who were becoming more frantic by the minute, surrounded the in-flight-services desk. They overheard everything going on, so the tension and the fear in the room were growing. I tried to stay focused on the tasks I needed to do as I once again scurried back to my manager Linda's desk. She needed to hear of Phil's call. It was the first official phone call reporting the hijacking of Flight 93.

Linda was on the phone with her superiors in Chicago when I interrupted her. She shared this new information with them at headquarters.

The flight attendants were still waiting for more information. Some were in the crew lounge, watching the horror on television, and others stayed at the desk with me. The calls continued to come faster than we could answer them.

I pulled up Flight 93 on my computer again. This time, the screen showed "Records Secure." That was all the confirmation I needed about their fate.

The National Guard or the Federal Aviation Administration (FAA)—I'm not sure which—ordered the evacuation of the airport. Almost immediately, buses pulled up to the door, and we loaded flight attendants onto them. I thought that this was a big event and we were in immediate danger.

The evacuation left just the office staff in our building to handle this situation. We had the guidance of our emergency manual under the section "Red Alert." We tried to follow the format of how to handle something like this, but how do you react to a hijacking by suicidal lunatics? There is not a plan to prepare you for something this horrific.

NATIONAL GUARD AND FBI

The National Guard arrived at the airport. They took up stations outside our office doors with guns and kept our area secure. No one could come or go. We now knew that the nation had suffered a terrorist attack.

Not long afterward, FBI agents showed up. They advised me on how to handle each call. These difficult calls came from fellow workers, family members of our crews, and flight attendants. Everyone wanted to find out which planes and which people had come under attack. The FBI gave us strict orders not to reveal any information about anything. That was most difficult because the flight attendants pled to me on the phone for any kind of answer. They knew that I knew more than I was saying. It was excruciating not to share the information with them.

The FBI showed up again in our office to question me. Two agents escorted my supervisor, Rob Perillo, and me upstairs to our management office. The walk through the airport was so odd with no passengers scurrying around or noises to hear. Everything was fairly quiet but heavily guarded by security forces and cops.

When we arrived upstairs, the agents found a room to sit me in. I heard all the chatter going on around me. I began to cry and could not stop. The full realization of what had happened caused me to lose it. Rob handled himself very professionally and tried to comfort me while I cried. He just held a box of tissues for me and stayed close.

It took me about fifteen minutes to be rational enough to even talk to the agents. They were gentle and patient. The female agent introduced herself as Jessie Esposito and said she worked with the terrorist task force. She asked the same questions over and over about the calls I had taken all morning. I repeated the answers over and over.

Jessie was very interested in the details of the calls. She wanted to know exactly what each caller said, who was on the line, how long the call lasted, and where it came from. The calls from Flight 93 and Phil Bradshaw were the agents' main interests.

The interview continued for a long time while government agents scurried about in all directions. Newark Airport was the last place I wanted to be at that moment. Jessie's male partner took notes as I sat through the long interview. Afterward, agents escorted me back to my desk at in-flight services.

ASSIGNMENTS FROM THE FBI

When I got back from talking to Jessie and her partner, other FBI agents were standing at my desk and monitoring the situation. The remaining office staff were receiving new assignments. My job was to stay on the phone. I had to answer and log every single call: the time, the caller, and the exact words they spoke to me. At the end of my day—which was about ten-thirty at night—I had about thirty pages of notes from telephone calls.

DUTIES AFTER

Incoming calls were a crucial source of information to us on 9/11. None of our phones, radios, or cell phones would dial out. We felt like we were in an underground bunker. In hindsight, we were, as there are no windows in our office and there is access to the ramp from our back door, with security alarms on the doors if they open. I tried to reach deep inside to find my own strength.

Linda MacDonald (the administrative secretary) and Thomas were assigned to relieve me on the phone when needed. We kept each other focused and struggled to get through the day. We tried to answer all the calls coming in and keep people calm. When the supervisor staff arrived around nine o'clock, they were all given duties as well.

Sallie got the job of locating the spouses of the pilots and flight attendants on Flight 93 because we knew they were in trouble. We needed to locate the spouses before they heard this information from elsewhere. The news would be devastating.

Thomas stayed with me on the phone lines, answering call after call and keeping people calm. Linda Duffey (the domicile manager) and Mary also took turns at the desk with us. It was a real team effort, as we were all scared to death.

STAFF AND MORE CALLS

Linda MacDonald (the administrative secretary) joined me at the desk and assisted with calls. Sallie, who was Linda's secretary, was also sent up front with me. We took turns crying and giving each other breaks from the phone calls.

Phil Bradshaw continued to call. We heard from him about three more times. Each call was more frantic than the last, asking us if we knew anything else about Sandy's flight. Every time we heard Phil's voice, his little boy, Nathan, was crying a bit louder in the background. Finally, on the last call, which came after the crash, Nathan was screaming. I am sure he sensed Phil's trouble and tension.

Thomas helped me through many hysterical moments that morning. Each time I lost my composure, he jumped in and calmed me down and took over the phone lines. Thomas was so calm that day, and I will always remember that. I thank God he was with me.

Thomas spoke to Phil several times. Thomas's voice was so calming that I am sure he didn't even realize how important he was that morning. He was a true blessing. I will never understand how he stayed so calm and professional. Thomas has a real talent for crises and people. I got a good look at his tender side, and I was very impressed.

LANDING AIRBORNE FLIGHTS

Now that all the staff had their duties, authorities ordered all flights to land immediately at the nearest airport. Air traffic came to a halt. We had many flights bound for Newark at that hour of the morning, and now they had to land wherever they were. Because there were so many airplanes in the air, many airports could not handle all those arrivals. For the safety of the planes, many diverted to Halifax, Nova Scotia, Canada.

The Canadians were so good to the Americans during 9/11, and Americans need to know that. Once all the hotels and airports filled up with American travelers, the citizens graciously opened their homes. We owe them a lot.

Many pilots and flight attendants stayed with Canadian families until they could come home. Some of our crews were stuck in Halifax for almost a week. It warms my heart to see that there are so many caring and compassionate people out there.

It was a grueling job trying to locate all our crews. There were no records anywhere, only incoming calls to give us information. It was mass confusion, especially while trying to handle the incoming calls from people who were sick with worry and praying for answers.

THE HORRIFIC BATTLE AND CRASH

The time in the office was going by slowly—as if it were a written script without an ending. The whole situation did not seem real as the office staff entered the office one by one and we relayed the news to them. By now we had all our supervisors there, and that was a relief to us. Any help would do.

Linda Staffieiri—one of the smartest and most professional supervisors on staff—had been overseeing the goings-on at the desk when I arrived in the office that morning. How things had changed since then! With grounded planes still arriving, flight attendants came downstairs at a constant pace. Each crew was more hysterical than the last. The faster they showed up, the faster the National Guard evacuated them.

Many of the phone calls now coming in were from crew members stranded at other bases and hotels. Most were just relieved to hear a familiar voice from their home base in Newark.

Finally, after hours of worry and complete confusion, a voice came over the airport system radio. It was Terry, our station manager, who oversaw the entire United staff. She said, "All managers, report to the crisis center." As soon as we heard that message, we knew that Flight 93 had crashed. We had been expecting that to happen, but nobody had had the nerve to bring it up.

Immediately many of us, including me, cried our eyes out. The guards outside our office door would not allow us to step out of the office. That was scary because it made us think that we were in danger, being stuck in the airport terminal. I just wanted out of that airport; I was really scared. Linda and Thomas covered for me while I took a couple of emotional moments for myself.

It seemed like forever that the management team was gone while we stayed on top of the incoming calls. We would tell the people on the other end that right now we did not know anything for sure but to stay calm. We would have to wait for United to give us information, and as they did, we would keep the callers informed. We told the family members of the crew to keep their phone lines open and wait for someone from United to contact them. Those were the most difficult calls to respond to. The FBI had told us not to reveal anything, even to family members.

Earlier, Sandy Bradshaw had called a couple of times from Flight 93. She said that Lorraine and Wanda were ministering to passengers. CeeCee was in the back galley with Sandy, preparing boiling water to fight the terrorists with. Sandy and I assumed that Debbie was already dead, along with the cockpit crew, Jason Dahl and LeRoy Homer.

I cannot even begin to describe how sickening those calls were to me. My emotions were beginning to crumble, although I tried not to show that to anyone. I knew how I was feeling inside, though. It was hard hearing from Sandy because I couldn't even imagine the fear and horror she and the others on board were experiencing.

As I write this five years later, I still have not been able to tell my full story to anyone, including my psychiatrist. I have severe anxiety when I go through it out loud. I am thankful that I can write about it. I find it important to remember everything from that day.

NOTIFICATION OF CRASH

At approximately eleven o'clock, our domicile manager, Linda Duffey, and the supervisors came back to the in-flight office. She told us to let the phones ring and asked everyone into a room next to the coordinator desk, where I was working. She took the phones off the hook and asked us all to sit down so that she could speak to us. There were approximately eight of us there at this point.

Linda said that Flight 93 had crashed in Shanksville, Pennsylvania and that there were no survivors. I remember feeling so sad, and the tears and hysterical sobbing hit me immediately. All of us sat there in that room for quite some time. We cried and had a few moments of silence for our friends on that flight. Someone led us in prayer. It was so emotional.

Linda was very gentle in breaking the news. We could see that the crisis center had trained her well on how to handle us. She asked each of us if we were okay and able to continue working. It took some time, but we all went back to our assigned duties. We were all anxious to return to our positions. Our colleagues needed us.

Sallie needed to quickly locate the crew's families so United representatives could break the awful news in person. She found everyone right away except for Eric Bay, Lorraine's husband. It took all day to locate Eric.

Joe, another supervisor and a good friend of Lorraine and Wanda, went to Wanda's home to notify her kids. Joe took it very hard.

Mary's duty was to try to find some means of communication and news updates in the office. We could not get the radios to work, so we didn't know what was going on out there. She was unsuccessful. So, we still relied on the news from the people calling us, mostly flight attendants.

SHOCKING CALL

A flight attendant named Kim Stroka called, and without even saying hello, she said, "Terry, who did I kill?" Although it stunned me to hear this, I really felt her pain. Kim was supposed to be on Flight 93 that morning, but she had something to attend with her daughter at school, so she had dropped the trip the night before. I believe Sandy Bradshaw had picked up the open slot on the flight. Kim cried her eyes out on the phone to me as I tried unsuccessfully to convince her not to feel guilty. She never flew again after that day.

Kim applied for disability and workers' compensation, but the system denied her and many others. The officials found that she wasn't on the job that day, so she wasn't qualified. I disagree wholeheartedly. Considering how my trauma and depression affected my life, I am sure the guilt that Kim felt just festered away at her soul.

A few months later, I called Kim, and she gave me the name of her lawyer, who is now my lawyer. With help from this attorney, Raymond Shebell, I won my case for workers' compensation.

NEWS FROM KATHY

Kathy, a flight attendant with many years of service with United, stands out in my mind as a true angel that day. Like me, she was very good friends with Wanda and Lorraine.

Kathy had September 11 off, so she watched the news from home. She called me about ten times that morning and kept updating me with information that we otherwise couldn't get. She did so much more than that, though. She kept me calm. Every time she called, she was very soothing to me. I am so grateful to Kathy and feel that I could never repay her for her compassion.

NJ TURNPIKE

By the end of 9/11, all the families of the Flight 93 crew had United employees at their homes. The employees helped them deal with their tremendous loss and grief.

I did manage to remain at my desk until late that evening. We had to be there; we were the main contact for our grounded crews all over the country. For some of them, we were their only source of information and contact. They needed us, and that was enough for me. I must say that it felt good to be their comforter on the other end of the phone.

I finally left the airport at about ten that night. It was difficult to leave. I had this sense of emptiness and wanted to remain in the airport to support the flight attendants. But I knew I needed to rest because they needed to hear a familiar voice on the line when they called us the next day.

To tell you the truth, I have no recollection of the drive home. I do remember my mom, my children, my mom's friend Anne Brown, and my then-husband, Jon Lowing, greeting me.

Even at home, the calls never stopped. Everyone who phoned me tried to get me to tell them who was on the flight that crashed. It was the most difficult thing to hide from them. The Flight 93 victims' names were not publicly released until a day or two later.

I watched CNN all night long and returned to the airport at six the next morning.

FAMILIES ALL NOTIFIED

Once all the crews' families had the difficult news, our crisis team spent some time with them. Then they were all driven to Newark, as air travel was still forbidden. It was very difficult to watch our supervisors go through this.

Kathy and Susan went to the crash site, where they met with some of the families. The airline met with all of them in a hotel in Newark to answer any questions they had. I cannot imagine the mood in that meeting room in those few days after 9/11.

MISSING SON OF A SUPERVISOR

As I review my writings, I am reminded of different times during the last few months of 2001. Rosemary Montgomery comes to mind. She was one of the onboard-service supervisors (and an ex-flight attendant). She was out flying to observe one of the crews, which was a supervisor's duty periodically. Rosie took the two-day trip to London with a 777 aircraft and was on her way home to land in Newark on the morning of 9/11.

Rosie's husband phoned and said that her son had work that day in the World Trade Center. He (the husband) hadn't heard anything about the son's whereabouts at that time. The concern must have been overwhelming. At that point, we still didn't even know where that 777 was. Rosie's husband asked us not to tell her about their son so she wouldn't be sick with worry.

We kept quiet while we all worried enough for Rosie that day. It was very difficult to know that her son may be dead or missing.

Rosie and her crew ended up in Canada for the next six days. Rosie called in several times, but we did not tell her. I think it was the right choice; we saved her a lot of anxiety and worry. There was nothing she could have done, anyway. We told her after they located their son, on the afternoon of 9/11. He was safe.

THE NEW YORK GIANTS

The New York Giants always charted United airplanes for their away games. They had the same crew work for all their flights. On 9/11, they got stuck in Denver when air travel stopped. They didn't make it back for a few days. Even when they landed in Newark, the airport officials didn't bring the plane to the gate or the jetway because they didn't want to take any chances. When they finally arrived, the football team rushed from the plane to a bus to the terminal and then evacuated.

MORE ALERTS

Every day, the flight attendants were advised to read the board hanging in the in-flight office as they entered. On this board were security alerts from the Federal Aviation Administration. In bright-red capital letters, they oftentimes began with "Al Qaeda Terrorist Alert."

FLIGHTS RESUME

The flights scheduled once air travel resumed shocked the industry. Lessened air traffic across the country became the new normal. After the traumatic events of 9/11, airlines had very few passengers. Flights were usually crewed with the newer reserve flight attendants. Nobody wanted to fly or work. These circumstances began to hurt United Airlines financially.

I heard many stories from the flight attendants who spoke with passengers traveling. The crews received heroes' greetings from passengers. With a newfound appreciation, travelers thanked our crews for working the trips. Crews were also showered with cards and flowers. For the longest time, the people on the aircraft cheered when the purser introduced the rest of the crew. The public saw them as heroes for getting back onto those planes. It took a lot of guts to work in the air after 9/11.

People are awesome when times are tough. They are supportive and there for each other. It was great for the flight attendants' morale.

AIR TRAVEL AND STRUGGLES BEGIN

I remember once flying started again, the agony of seeing the crews coming with such pain and fear of flying. After all, nobody felt safe at this point. Can you imagine getting on a plane to go to work after all this? Within one week of the terror, our office filled with mental-health workers specializing in trauma. Most were with the Red Cross. I cannot begin to tell you how amazing they were.

One man who touched my life during this time was Randy Prescott. He was from somewhere out West, I believe, and he came to Newark to help. His specialty was trauma and post-traumatic stress. Randy talked me through many tough days on the job following 9/11. He urged me several times to take some downtime as well; of course, I never listened until it was too late.

Many of the captains were also incredible during the first few weeks. They sat with the crews and attended their briefings and tried to assure them of their safety. They showed the flight attendants that they were not alone and calmed the fears of many.

Jim Taylor, one of our captains, and his wife, Hillary, dedicated so much time to our office. They were truly concerned with our crews. Jim, as a captain, assured the flight attendants that they were safe. He said that all the pilots wouldn't be flying if they felt any differently.

Each day, Jim asked for a list of the flights and check-in times. He wanted to attend the flight attendants' briefings and advise the crews of new safety measures coming from the pilots. Jim and Hillary were a great team and gave countless hours. They also touched me with their pep talks and compassion.

WEEKS AFTER

When I arrived at the office on September 12, which was Wednesday, I was not the main coordinator on the desk. Debby Coniglio was the morning worker that day. The calls were still coming in constantly, so two people on the phones were necessary.

The flight attendants who called that day still frantically asked which of their colleagues had died. The computer had locked out that information, so we were their only source to contact. It was hard not to be able to tell the flight attendants the information they were looking for. The names were not yet released officially.

After the crew and passenger names became public, the calls became more difficult. We consoled each other and speculated about what had happened on Flight 93.

The first week went by slowly and soberly, as the airport was still closed. We mainly dealt with scheduling on those days to try to get all our displaced crews back home again. Most finally arrived back in Newark on Friday or Saturday.

There was still a lot of security around our office door because our back door had access to the ramp where the aircraft was located. With the airport closed, it was quite eerie. Many Port Authority police and investigators from the FAA, FBI, and National Guard were there. The only other employees in the airport were some American Airlines employees because two of their planes were also involved in the attacks.

Linda MacDonald (the administrative secretary) worked countless hours, staying until late on the night of September 11 and returning at six the next morning. The next few days were a blur to me. One afternoon later that week, all the victims' names aired on television. Now, with a sense of finality, it was time to deal with the grief everyone felt.

We had approximately eight hundred flight attendants based out of Newark at the time. Two hundred of them were just hired in November 2000, CeeCee Lyles being one of them.

EMPLOYEES' WORDS

Soon after the initial shock of everything wore off, I began journaling. In October 2001, I sent a system-wide email to the flight attendants to ask if they would like to share with me their stories of their terror on that day. I received a huge response.[2]

Below is the letter I sent:

Hello, lovely flight attendants:

I am working on a project about 9/11/01 and Flight 93. I would like to share some of your stories in my documents. I realized that some things were not clear in my mind from that day, and I do not want to miss anything. I always want to remember, so I will be documenting everything for our five crew members who died as heroes. Please email me with your comments if you wish. Thank you so much for your love and constant support to each other and me.

Love,
Your in-flight coordinator, Terry Horniacek Lowing

The responses came back quickly.

Desiree Paulius:
Hi, Terry,
Around seven a.m. on 9/11, I was in the V position on a 757 landing at Newark. Flight attendant Holly Marshall was our purser.

---

[2] Letters have been edited for clarity and brevity.

Flight 93 used the 757 after we landed and deplaned. Their crew was waiting for us at the gate because we were late by about a half hour. I went to the flight attendant lounge to nap before commuting back home, but then all hell broke loose. Supervisor Eileen Ammiano told the three of us in the lounge to turn the television on, and I fell back to sleep, not paying attention. I woke up alone in the lounge. Eileen came in again and told me I must evacuate the airport. Thanks for asking, and feel free to contact me for more details if you would like. I've seen a lot in my life, but this was the saddest day of them all.

Lisa Butler:

Hi, Terry,

I arrived at the domicile at about five a.m. Gayle Kamei, Gino Pasquale, and C. J. Marsh were working Flight 81 with me. We were going to Los Angeles. As I walked through the terminal, I noticed that the Muslim men were not praying toward Mecca in the airport that morning. This was odd because every morning they were there, on their knees and barefoot, facing the window in prayer. I remember seeing Linda Catania (another flight attendant), and we walked down to the office together. I saw CeeCee Lyles coming out of the crew lounge and waved to Lorraine Bay, who was coming down the escalator as we were going up.

I also vividly remember a conversation with you about which shift you liked to work. You said that in the mornings we are usually too quiet and that the real action was at night. How ironic. You said that you were covering because Debby was sick, and it was normally her shift. When we got to our aircraft, we saw Barbara Upperman on the airplane before we left. We later diverted to Lincoln, Nebraska, and saw the events unfold from downstairs in their operations center for a while before getting hotel rooms downtown.

Karen Hecker:

Terry, before I say anything, I must say that you are loved and respected by so many in our domicile. You are our smile when we leave and our smile when we return. Thank you, dear one, Terry.

I was home on that horrible day in Pittsburgh. I need to tell you in person the events that took place, so please feel free to call me or catch me in the domicile. Sandy Bradshaw was one of my crash-pad roomies that were never there. An ideal roomie, like we all called her. I had a difficult time reading her name on the calendar in our room after 9/11. I'll gladly share the memories I have of that trying event when I return to work in eleven days, hopefully after our initial pain.

Roy Vickeroy:

In Denver, while waiting for our departure to Newark, I watched the New York Giants arrive. We made it forty-five minutes outside of Denver after a 6:15 a.m. departure. Then, we turned around and got booked into a hotel, where we held up until Saturday. We were originally coming home on Thursday morning.

Joie Karnes:

Hey, Terry,

I didn't look to see that this was from you until I read your second note. How are you? I haven't seen you for a while. How are you and your husband and kids doing? Great, I hope?

On 9/11, I was in San Diego, getting ready to come home through Denver, when my other flight attendant on the crew knocked on my hotel-room door and said, "We aren't going anywhere." She turned the television on, and we watched the second tower fall. I called my husband (then of only two weeks), the bond trader, who thought for one hour and forty minutes that he had seen me fly into one of those buildings, where all his friends worked as

44

well. After calling family to let them know we were fine, we kept tuned in to the television. During the afternoon, the San Diego staff organized a meeting place for those of us staying in the hotel, where they answered what questions they could. I explained my situation and that I was going into vacation time. My husband was really upset and wanted me home. A supervisor there helped to release me from duty so that I could drive back to New Jersey. I met my husband in Iowa, and we traveled home to Jersey together. I hope to see you soon.

    -Joie

Peggy Smith:

Hi, Terry,

I was one of your standby people on September 11. It was my first day back from an occupational injury (bus accident in London). Three briefings were going on at the same time. I was reading my mail, thinking that I was going to San Fran[cisco] because the Flight 93 crew kept asking, "Where's Wanda?" You continued to tell them that she would come. Sure enough, about ten minutes into their briefing, Wanda came rushing in. She had green AFA [Association of Flight Attendants, a union] bag tags and passed them out to everyone. Mine is on my bag as a reminder that no day is a bad day and to take time to enjoy each day because life is so short.

I went to the flight attendants' lounge and fell asleep. About a half hour later, you woke me up, saying, "Sorry, girls, there has been a crash." I turned the television back on, and we watched the second plane go into the tower, and shortly after, our television reception went out.

We all moved to the counter in front of your desk. You were on the phone and said, "I hope one of those planes wasn't ours." Everything was quiet. I said, "I wish we could see what was going on [meaning on TV]," and someone said, "Go to the ticket counter upstairs, and you can see it all." I went outside for a while and came back in. By that time, they were evacuating the airport. I caught the employee bus to drive home.

The parkway was like a parking lot. People had pulled to the side of the road and were standing by their cars, watching the towers. Later, I was watching television, and they identified the crash in Pennsylvania as one of our own, United Flight 93. At that time, the authorities released no names or information. I didn't realize right away that it was a San Francisco flight. If it had been anyone but Wanda, I would have been the one on that flight. I obviously have something else to do here, so I'm being patient and enjoying every day. I've thought about writing notes to my relatives to tell them my most memorable times spent with each of them. That's one of my short-term goals.

Love,

Peggy

Kathleen Allen-Dawe:

Hi, Terry,

I've been thinking of you, especially over the last month. I've reconnected my computer, and there was your email about the events of 9/11. I wrote a paper on that day, and I broke it up as the minutes evolved. I just recently moved to Wall, and Bob and I have officially blended families. I am so thankful for the time off on many different fronts. I hope you are doing well. I'm afraid I have lost your phone number in the move. Please give me a call, as I would love to see you and get caught up. My best to you always.

Love,

Kathy

Betty Veit:

Dear Terry,

I arrived at six-thirty a.m. on 9/11 and went into the computer room. I was catching a flight at 7:15 for training in Chicago. I sat down next to Debbie Welsh, and we chatted. I said, "Your hair looks pretty," and she replied that she was letting it grow. I asked if they got the apartment they were looking at. Debbie said no and that there had been a problem with subletting. She asked how Taylor was, and I asked where she was going. She replied, "San Francisco at eight o'clock," and I told her to have a good trip and said goodbye. So sad.

Betty

Donna Jones:

Sorry, Terry, I cannot help you but to say where I was that morning. We diverted to Halifax, Nova Scotia, that day, originally coming back from London. We landed and sat on the runway in Canada for approximately four hours before authorities allowed us to deplane and undergo a search by dogs and agents. Then we proceeded through their customs and into their lounge. Afterward, they arranged for us to stay at a hotel—however, we did not know that the length of our stay would be until Friday.

Donna Jones

Alicia Sommer:

Hi, honey,

I was not there, but I think of you often and how your day must have been. I admire your courage and love for everyone, and I do not think I could have done as well as you did. I hope those memories are not haunting to you and that someday you will think of them as just that—memories. Thinking of you always.

Love,
Alicia

Elsa Esteves:

Dear Terry,

What a beautiful email, and yes, we will get through these horrific months. You know I will always be here for you, no matter what time of day or night. I feel that you were an angel sent to us at Newark, and we cannot do it without you. Because of your courage, your strength, compassion, kindness, and love—you, my friend, are truly a blessing! You have touched my life, and I thank you for loving me the way you do. You are a hero. You are an angel. A big hug is coming your way with lots of love and gratitude for all you have done.

Your friend,
Elsa

The Newark flight attendants are a beautiful bunch of people. They are very supportive of each other and care so much for the next guy. They proved it all over again when I had a mental breakdown in 2002 (which I will discuss later in this book). I looked back in March 2003 at all the letters and well wishes I received, and I am touched to tears. It reminds me of how much I desperately miss my friends and my job in Newark. I often pull out the phone list that I took when I left. I read over their names and phone numbers, and I keep saying I want to call them and never do. It is a very difficult place for me to go emotionally.

As I read through my journals and continue to write, I realize that I am healing over time. It has probably taken me much longer than many, but I am improving with each September 11 that passes. The doctors think that I have had many devastating life events in the five years since that day, so it will take time. They also tell me I will always carry that trauma with me through life. I will just learn healthier ways to deal with it.

In October 2002, I received this letter signed by hundreds of flight attendants:

Dear Terry:

It has been one year since September 11, 2001. We had a lot of time to think of the important things in life. One of those things that came to mind was the people that matter, and of course, you came to mind. We want to thank you for being there for us on September 11, 2001. You have been human enough to realize that we were terrified and needed people to hold our hands and lead us back to work. You gave us that gentle push. You listened to us venting our fears and concerns. Sometimes that is what we needed most.

Please accept this letter as a heartfelt thank-you. Saying thank you is not enough for all the nice things you have done for us and all the times you have been there for us. But once again, thank you, and keep doing what you have been doing. We notice.

Yours very truly . . .

SHERATON MEMORIAL SERVICE

In December 2001, our office planned a memorial service for the crew of Flight 93 because their home base was in Newark. It took place at the Sheraton Hotel at Newark Airport. It was a service for all the airline employees. I think over five hundred people attended the service. We asked the Boys Choir of Harlem and the New York City Fire Department to be our guests.

The Sheraton created an elegant setup. Outside the memorial room was a huge area filled with photos of the Flight 93 crew with their families. Debbie Welsh had her Dalmatian with her in one of her photos. She looked beautiful.

That meeting place outside the room was very difficult to look at. Everywhere I looked, I saw blue from the uniforms the flight attendants wore. Everyone had pins tacked on their clothes.

You see, there were a lot of pins made up for the employees. Many of the employees had the idea to raise money for the Flight 93 fund for their families. We sold angels with wings with *UA 93* and *9-11* inscribed on the front. Our office made ribbons with the red and blue colors of United. Whatever was available, we all bought them and wore them proudly. I wore six pins that day. I received Flight 93 decals for my car and several angels and 9/11 pins from flight attendants. I have them all in a box where I keep all the keepsakes from that tragic time.

We all gathered while waiting and comforted each other and the family members. I distinctly remember going inside for a seat. Attendees packed the huge room. There was a huge movie screen and a podium up front with flags hanging from the stage. As I walked into the room, I was a little freaked out because I finally had to confront these deaths for real. I was concentrating hard on controlling my emotions. I tried not to hear the speakers when they went up front. Sandy Dahl was one of them. Her husband, Jason, was the captain of Flight 93.

My coworkers from the office were all sitting together in a row in the back. I wasn't quite comfortable with them, to tell the truth. I felt like my closest friends and support system were the flight attendants. They must have agreed because as I went to sit with the other coordinators and supervisors, flight attendants Elsa Esteves and Brendan Corbalis called me to their row. They had saved room for me right in the middle of all the crew members.

At that moment, the flight attendants were stirring in their seats. I soon learned why, as Linda Duffey (our domicile manager) came up behind me and said, "Terry, the office staff is sitting in a row in the back. These seats are for the flight attendants."

Brendan said to her, "She is one of us. Terry can stay right here."

And so, I did just that.

Word quickly spread of what Linda had said, and the flight attendants were all ticked off. There was a lot of talk about her trying to move me away from them. Brendan and Elsa whispered to me that the flight attendants all wanted me with them through this. I was very touched by that. They said they had appreciated me during the last few weeks. It was at least comforting to me.

At that time, I did not feel I was part of the office staff anymore. I felt a distance from some of them. I believe some of them resented the bond the flight attendants and I had. We became very close throughout this tragedy.

I was feeling quite alone before I walked into that room. When I turned around to see the office staff, some were looking at me. I am sure there were comments made. The next couple of months in the office were tough.

Elsa held a box of tissues on her lap when the service began. We held hands, and many sobbed. The Boys Choir of Harlem sang "Amazing Grace." It was soul-stirringly beautiful. Everyone in the room sat completely still. It was moving to hear these children sing.

The fire department provided the color guard. The members did a somber march with their flags up the aisle toward the front of the room. The choir's patriotic song brought tears to my eyes. On the screen up front, pictures of the crew flashed constantly. I sat through the speeches and pictures. I was even okay through the pictures on the wall as the flight attendants around the room wept.

When the choir sang "Wind Beneath My Wings," I practically ran out. I found a corner where I could be alone and have a good cry. Pete Prescott from the Red Cross found me and comforted me. Then Rob Perillo, my supervisor, came out, and a couple of flight attendants followed.

I think the song hit home for me, as it was my grandmother's favorite and we had played it for her funeral the year before. That day was the first time I had felt the full pain of the 9/11 losses and tragedy.

RED CROSS ASSISTANCE

I find it odd that I currently cannot work, because for the months right after the crashes, I worked fifty-to-sixty-hour weeks with flight attendants who still tried to work their schedules. Many of them came in nervous and leery of working their trips. I assisted with putting many of them on sick leave and helped many of them to counsel with the Red Cross, whose representatives came to our office every day for months after the attacks. Some of the flight attendants just went through the motions, as did I.

The Red Cross did a wonderful job, and I cannot give them enough praise. People trained in trauma and crisis came to us from all over the country. They provided a lot of counseling to our staff for many weeks.

I remember one man in particular, Randy Prescott, who on so many different occasions warned me about "crashing." He advised me many times to slow down and take some mental-health time for myself. He always said he could see me draining myself emotionally. I never took the advice, but he was right.

On January 17, 2002, I had a mental breakdown. I dropped as if a ton of bricks had hit me. I could do nothing useful for myself, my job, or my family.

UNION AND VOLUNTEER SUPPORT

United Airlines' Newark crews were compassionate and volunteered to help their coworkers. Many union representatives came to that office day after day, meeting with flight attendants before they flew. These reps attended briefings and coached the flight attendants through their fears and grief. They also assisted with signing out of work for the ones who were too devastated to fly.

Jason King and Patti Price, two of the union representatives, were so dedicated during this time. They were both so calming and professional as they comforted everyone who came in. Patti and Jason were wonderful to me, and I will always have a place in my heart for them. I feel that way about so many of the flight attendants. They were so dedicated and there for me and each other. They truly cared and worked countless hours in that in-flight office.

I received this letter after I was out on disability along with about two hundred get-well cards.

UNION HELP AND THE SPIRIT ROOM

Mary Lou Phippin was the representative from the union employee assistance program (EAP). This program helped any flight attendant who suffered some loss or tragedy in their life. Mary Lou helped refer many of the employees to counseling. I phoned her on several occasions on behalf of flight attendants who were an emotional mess.

I felt like a therapist working full time. For the first few months after the crash, I listened to painful stories all day, every day. The flight attendants and I bonded so much over this horror. Still, it drained me emotionally.

Mary Lou was very compassionate to me when I was sick at home with my breakdown. She phoned me all the time and was truly an angel during my time of depression. Karen Mazeur, another union officer, spent countless hours in the office helping crews and me get through the sadness and trauma.

The weeks went by. One room in the office slowly turned into a shrine decorated with love shown for the Flight 93 crew. We all cherished it. First, flowers covered the desk. They were from flight attendants and other airline employees. Some came from families of flight attendants. Some came from employees from the merchants in the airport. We received pictures and beautifully engraved plaques. As each gift arrived, we put it in the chosen room. We even received a plaque from the White House. Kathy Collis made an album of all the photos and newspaper articles. It was a truly beautiful way to honor our lost friends.

The room is now called the Spirit Room. I used to call it the Death Room because I would walk the long way around instead of walking through it. It was too difficult for me to look at for quite some time.

CAUSE FUNDRAISER

At United, the CAUSE (Concerned Attendants for a United Support Effort) program had existed for some time to raise funds for employees in need during a crisis. Run by United attendants, it helps support ill crew members and the children of deceased flight crews. For example, one lady had her house burn down, and the CAUSE funds assisted her. Everyone at United had the option to have money deducted from their paychecks and put toward the program.

Just a few months after the attacks, the CAUSE program planned a fundraiser for the families of our crew on Flight 93. The organizers decided to hold a banquet and a silent auction.

CAUSE members all pulled whatever strings we could and worked on soliciting stores and restaurants for donations for the fundraiser. Everyone I called proved more than willing to donate. A band volunteered their time. Laura Layton, one of the flight attendants, and her husband owned a Mexican restaurant in South Jersey, so they offered to host the event and donate the food. All the items for the silent auction also came from donations.

The vendors and donors showed amazing generosity. The fundraiser raised over $50,000. It warmed my heart to see the employees work so hard on such a great cause.

This fundraiser became an annual event. In 2002, we held it at the Stirling Hotel in North Jersey. The flight attendants once again worked as a real team to raise over $40,000. Hopefully, this event will continue in the Newark domicile every year. The money will surely help the families of our employees and friends who lost their lives.

From October through December 2001, I worked a lot of overtime at the airport. Having my husband, Jon, and the kids at home also took its toll on me. I began to take days off frequently and started to feel depressed and burned out. This became apparent to me when I started crying at work almost daily. I think I had so much bottled up, and every time I talked to the flight attendants, trying to console them, I would end up crying.

Our domicile manager, Linda Duffey, scheduled a mental-health briefing for the employees in our office. She wanted to make sure we had help for dealing with our grief and the trauma of it all. The company shrink came as part of the event.

However, I didn't know about any of this until afterward. To my surprise, I came to work one day and found out that this mental-health briefing had happened on my day off. I had worked the desks on 9/11. Wouldn't it have made sense for me to attend the briefing? I hope that Linda just overlooked me.

I did see Judy Klein, our company shrink, during work time one morning. Her advice to me was to get away from the airport for a while. She said to give myself some time to focus on my emotions and time to feel the trauma and grief. She sent the recommendation to my boss, Linda Duffey, but I felt as if Judy were wrong. I thought I was okay and could handle things. I did not want to be away from the flight attendants right now. I wouldn't have stayed home, so it was useless to recommend that to me.

I became involved with the planning of funerals, fundraisers, and recovery efforts. I felt I needed to be with the flight attendants. Most of the staff felt as I did, so we all worked overtime, mostly consoling each other and doing lots of planning. There was so much to think about at this point. Everything ended up coming together beautifully, and I give so much credit to the United Airlines flight attendants for the efforts and love they put into every task in those difficult times.

UAL LOSES MONEY AND EMPLOYEES

After 9/11, United Airlines was quickly losing money, like the other airlines. We were just going broke quicker, along with American Airlines, because of our companies' involvement in the crashes. United and the employees received government assistance, but it just wasn't enough.

I watched three different sets of furloughs completely break down our employee morale. It was such a difficult time for everyone, including United itself. The flights soon became fewer and fewer each day. Work began to get a bit boring with so few passengers and so much time between flight-attendant check-ins. Morale and our company pocketbooks were dwindling in real time.

HOLIDAYS 2001

As December approached, we were trying to somehow lift the spirits of those still coming to work every day and flying. I decided to decorate the office for Christmas. I went crazy with lights, balls, and garlands. The office looked like Rockefeller Center at Christmas. It turned out festive, with real warmth about it.

I cannot tell you how many flight attendants thanked me. That little bit of spirit and peaceful feeling helped the mood in the office. Before Christmastime, it was very dark and difficult to walk in and face the memories. With approval to spend some petty cash and some of my own money, I bought one hundred dollars' worth of holiday decorations. The two days it took to finish were truly worth it. At least we could come in and have our spirits filled with holiday joy and love instead of grief and fear at work. Too many of us remained in a struggle with the memory and pain of that horrific day.

Christmas 2001 had become the most difficult I had ever experienced. I had to work the morning shift, so I had planned an afternoon brunch with my family. I didn't mind working, because I would be there with a flight attendant and one of the supervisors. I was home by one p.m., and Jon, my husband, had most of the food set up when I arrived. We had our house very festive, and there were tons of gifts under the tree for the kids, as there always were.

I think the kids and my mom saw right through my seemingly happy smile. Deep down, I was dying with depression and grief. I just couldn't make it go away. Those dark thoughts were continually swirling in my headspace, my psyche—and my soul. Regardless, I got through the day and then my birthday and then New Year's. I was so glad to see the year end.

SHANKSVILLE

Those Americans on Flight 93 decided that they would fight that morning; they would die in the battle. The Somerset County coroner, Wallace Miller, calls this crash site "hallowed ground," a cemetery. The Borough of Shanksville and Stonycreek Township have taken on the job of being caretakers to the site. People from everywhere, including United Airlines flight attendants, have visited the site of the crash. It has been a national memorial site since 2002. Barbara Black, the memorial's now-retired chief of cultural resources, helped preserve the items left at the site. For a while there would be roughly five to six thousand people visiting the site per week, most leaving memorabilia.

Federal authorities have identified all passengers and crew from Flight 93. About one hundred and fifty volunteers took part in a final sweep of the property in May 2002, looking for human remains or personal property. Then there were still items found by the coroner that was no bigger than a matchbook. With DNA samples from the families, the authorities confirmed all identities.

I interviewed Barbara Black by phone in 2001. She states that this crash is a nationwide event. It is evident by the things people are leaving as memorials or just to show their respect for the site. Barbara felt it was extremely important to preserve every item, as you would for a museum. All items have also been computer cataloged with images. By 2002, the Shanksville site's memorabilia filled two full rooms. Each day, volunteers in the township collected these items to save as a part of history.

The town also has begun a volunteer program. Locals act as ambassadors to greet the thousands of people visiting the site. The Shanksville mayor, Ernest Stull, and his wife have been among the town's volunteers. United Airlines flight attendants have provided group bus trips to the site each year on the anniversary date. They have also provided trips to gate 11 in Newark Airport, from which Flight 93 left that day.

Some may say, "Let it go and move on." If you are saying that, then you surely do not understand the impact these crew members and passengers have had on America. They are truly my idols, my heroes. I never want the nation to forget them. Shanksville certainly will never let their memory die.

In February, Coroner Miller organized a meeting for the family members of the crew and passengers. On February 23, 2002, thirty-six of the forty family members were present. The families bonded at that first meeting, held in a hotel in Newark. They arrived as strangers, and they left each other as family. Miller gave them all a chance to meet and help finalize plans for the memorial at the crash site. In March, he met with them again to return any personal items that search parties had found.

THE FIFTH ANNIVERSARY

We are now coming up on the fifth anniversary of 9/11, and I continue to heal and deal with the post-traumatic stress those events have left with me. I have not worked since December 2002 and have had to rely on workers' compensation, as I probably will for the rest of my life. I tried to go back to work three different times, but the anxiety grew so strong that my doctor signed me out of work for good.

FIVE YEARS LATER

Today is September 11, 2006, exactly five years after the terrorist attacks. I am still frequently seeing a psychiatrist and taking many medications. I find myself glued to the news, watching all the coverage on the memorials being held. I am wishing so badly that I was in Shanksville right now, honoring my friends on Flight 93. I know deep in my heart it is probably not a good idea to be there, because the trauma is still so fresh for me. I find myself at the doctors searching for answers. Why is this so fresh in my mind today, and why can't I get rid of the fear and anxiety I suffer so greatly?

I had a visit with the psychiatrist three days before the anniversary date, and he said something to me about what to do with myself on the fifth anniversary. I was so torn about whether to attend a memorial or just put the whole day out of my mind. He said, "You already know the end result, probably better than most people know, so what will you get from attending?" I cried during my visit with him because the anxiety was so great over the coming day.

I decided in the end not to go to Shanksville and not to watch the memorials on television and just tried to act like it was just another day. I must say it was very difficult, though. I did participate in the moments of silence on television during the morning, but I stayed away from all the other media coverage. I did, however, find that on that day, I felt more alone than normal. Maybe *alone* isn't the word—*vulnerable*, perhaps. Overall, I was not in a good state of mind, taking Xanax all day just to stay calm throughout. But anyway, I made it through 9/11/06.

PART II: 9/11'S RESOUNDING ECHOES IN MY LIFE

Sometimes I feel as if I am a comforting person who needs to love others and feel needed. This is especially rewarding when I feel that my kids are open to my love. I have a lot to make up for with my children, and I do not know if I can ever do that. I certainly want to.

For a while, I took care of my ninety-year-old grandfather every day because he couldn't stay home by himself. It provided me a lot of healing because my deceased mom had played a big part in his life. I felt as if I did her job by filling her shoes. On the other hand, maybe I have had these chances to help my loved ones to make up for the things I have done.

I worry a lot because I understand what I want to do and the kind of person I want to be, but sometimes I cannot. I fall into depression or manic moods. I get off track and confused and often overwhelmed, then I disappoint my loved ones. So, what do I do then? I write in my journal, I try to plead my case, and I ask for forgiveness.

I beg the Lord to keep me sane, but I know I have a lot of issues. Maybe I will never resolve them, but I will never stop trying. I regret the life I have led because I have never been responsible like my mother. I feel as if I never had the skills. Even though I watched her work her butt off and get a nursing degree and provide her children with everything, I could never measure up to her mothering.

I feel the hurt and pain I have brought my kids through. It was never intentional, of course, but they walked a rough road. Other times I feel like a piece of garbage who cannot love or mother my children because of a lack of self-care. At those times, I cannot seem to pull myself out of a slump, and that often goes along with feeling rejected and sorry for myself.

This is the reason I have labeled myself as codependent. In the past, I believed I could not survive on my own. In fact, I never had to because of bad choices that I made with relationships so I could always feel loved or protected. For example, I would jump from one toxic relationship to another just so I wouldn't be alone.

Pretty pathetic, I know. I want so badly to trust in myself and stand on my own, but I feel most of the time that I cannot. This codependency issue is a big one and often goes along with self-destruction and addictions.

This quote about self-perception has stuck with me: "A balanced view of ourselves will help us better understand our shortcomings while also giving us greater hope in our potential."[3]

---

[3] Stephen Arterburn, David Stoop. *The Life Recovery Bible NLT Large Print Edition.* (Carol Stream, IL: Tyndale House, 2018), 5, https://www.google.com/books/edition/Life_Recovery_Bible_NLT_Large_Print /00_cDwAAQBAJ?hl=en&gbpv=1&dq=%E2%80%9C.

DIAGNOSIS PTSD

I began writing memoirs of my life as my troubles seemed to overwhelm me. Writing has always proven therapeutic to me. Now, so many years later, I find myself finally dealing with grief and pain that I had never really faced, but tried to move on from. The day of 9/11 has changed my life forever. Those events severely shook my life and mental stability. I felt as if my whole world came crashing down around me. I became sick and isolated for a long time. I had to face things that I could never do before.

KIDS

The most precious thing by far in my life is my children. They have walked through this journey with me. My children have been my strength when I have allowed them to be. They understand me more than I know myself sometimes. They have shown me as much compassion and love as anyone could deserve. They are my life and my reason for living.

- Kristen Marie Wombough, born 1986
- Jason Paul Wombough, born 1987
- Kathleen Ann Wombough, born 1989
- Donald Walter Pfirman, born 1992

While writing this book, I have to introduce my kids and tell each of their stories. They have each played such a significant part in my life, and I need them to know that if they do not already.

Kristen is strong, driven, and loving. Everyone would say she has a beautifully sweet, compassionate nature. I, of course, as her mother, have to agree. Nothing stops her from achieving what she is after. I really admire her. I feel I have the same characteristics, but I have always stopped myself from fully developing them.

Kristen works hard. As a teenager, since she was about fourteen, she worked every weekend and used her own money for clothes and spending. At the same time, she carried straight A's in school and earned the love of her teachers and coaches. She is athletically talented as well.

Kristen seems to succeed at everything she tries. I cannot express my pride in her, never mind my gratitude for her years of love and friendship to me when I needed her. She has always stood up for her younger brothers and sister with every bit of energy she has. Kristen has her standards, and she does not compromise them for anyone. I think that is what makes me so proud to be her mother. I could have taken lessons from her in my life.

How ironic that my choices have taught my daughter to be a better person in her own life. She was born in Red Bank, New Jersey, and of course, was immediately the sunshine in our lives, being the only baby. My family just adored her. She had bright red hair and a chubby little body. We knew she was brilliant when she started walking at eight and a half months old and talking very early.

I was twenty-one when Kristen was born, and she was by my side throughout the journey I call my lost and confused life. That kid stood by her mom no matter what the circumstances were. She was a tough little thing from the beginning. She used to fight with the girls who tried to bully her during her elementary-school years. It was a rough neighborhood, and she backed down from nobody. Kristen always protected her younger brothers and sister without hesitation.

As a teenager, Kristen attended Keansburg High School in New Jersey. She was always popular. Our house was always the hangout for the neighborhood kids. At about seventeen, Kristen started having some problems and showing self-destructive behavior. This was no surprise, considering the instability she had experienced in her life. This was not the fault of anyone but me, her mother.

Unfortunately, I never saw this until recently. It never even dawned on me that we were so dysfunctional. It was all known, I guess, so I didn't see it. It probably had a lot to do with my crazy relationship with my father all the years of my growing up and adult life. But when the lights went on in my head and I kept writing, I saw what a sick pattern I was repeating. Despite everything she has seen, Kristen is a well-balanced woman and couldn't love me more despite my faults.

Kristen (who lost one little girl, Hannah, just after birth) has three children: Nikolas, Jackson, and Emily. She raises them with her boyfriend, Kevin, who also has a son, Seth. I love them all dearly.

Jason, or Jay, is my second child, who is brilliant in athletics. He has always excelled in football. He played peewee at the age of five and has played football all his life. He was always a big kid, and he used to run laps with garbage bags wrapped around him to make weight to play for Pop Warner. He was also very driven.

Jay was the nurturer of all the children and was my emotional support during many of my difficult times. When I went through my depression after 9/11, Jason would lie with me on the couch, wipe my tears, and tell me, "Mama, don't cry." He was always so compassionate—my big mush. Jason went to football camp at Combine for the scouts to go pro, but he got hurt during tryouts. He had twelve NFL teams looking at him. I suppose God had another path for him.

Today, Jason is a teacher and an outstanding trainer. He is a football coach and director of football operations and coaches NFL athletes. I cannot tell you how proud I am of Jason. He won the Vince Lombardi Award in high school and has had many other great achievements in football. My addiction consumed me, but Jason's foster father, Don Pfirman, was always present for his accomplishments. I am so grateful for Don today and have so much respect for him as a man, as he never, ever turned his back on my children. He was more than a great father; he was an incredible role model. The kids love Don very much, and so do I.

Jay married his high-school sweetheart, Leanne. They have two beautiful boys, Jason and Jacob, whom I love deeply.

Katie is my third baby and so beautiful. She is a lot like me in her temperament. Her name comes from my mother, Kathleen Ann, and it's amazing that she turned out to look just like Mom. Katie also is very driven, like her sister, as she stops at nothing to succeed.

In 2011, Katie fell off a golf cart while vacationing on the West Coast. She suffered severe skull fractures and bleeding and swelling on the brain. I'll never forget the phone call from the hospital. It was a Thursday. They said, "Get here. She is in a coma." It was devastating. Don and the other kids and I sat at her bedside, which seemed like forever.

Katie, through God's grace, eventually recovered, but it was a rough road. She needed a lot of occupational and physical therapy. She went on to get her associate's and bachelor's in criminal justice at Brookdale and Rutgers. Today she works for the Department of Children and Families. She is also in a loving relationship with Robbie Misura, a UPS driver. It thrills me to see Katie so happy. I hope they get married and have a great big family someday. Katie so wants children, and she will make a great mom, as she is so loving, caring, and compassionate.

Donnie is my youngest baby, who stands at about six feet, four inches, and is beautiful. He is great with kids and is single. He has an air-conditioning and heating business with his father out of South Jersey. It has proven very successful. Donnie is good at what he does.

When Donnie was small, he was very sick with asthma. He ended up in the hospital probably more than thirty times before he was five. His lungs were so bad. Don and I took turns sleeping at the hospitals. Donnie had several surgeries at a young age, too. It was heartbreaking, but I am happy to say my son grew out of asthma over the years and is healthy today, thank God.

Donnie and I were at odds for many years because of my addiction and broken promises over the years. He was hurt and bitter. It took a long time to heal. But today, my relationship with all my children is beautiful. It's all thanks to my twelve-step program,

God, and doing the right thing daily. I have found peace and serenity, and I think my kids see that.

The twelve-step program has saved me in many ways. When I first walked in, several women embraced me with love, compassion, and support. They seemed to know me and my story. I felt as if I belonged. I had found my home there.

One woman in particular, who was speaking to the group, later approached me and said, "Here is my phone number. Call me anytime." Her name is Melanie Straniero. I thought there was no way I was going to call her because I didn't even know her. But that is how we stay clean, one day at a time: by reaching out to others and using their experience, strength, and hope.

So, I called Melanie. Today she is my sponsor in the program. She guides me through working on the twelve steps of recovery. She supports me through everything in my daily life, and she is my number-one fan. I don't know where I'd be without her. She is truly a role model to me, and I believe my deceased mother had a hand in sending her to me. She is family, and I love her so much. I owe my recovery to her.

ADMIT TO RIVERVIEW

In January 2002, I was admitted to Riverview Hospital in Red Bank, New Jersey. The staff immediately sent a psychiatrist to sedate me. They then admitted me to the psychiatric floor, which I only vaguely remember because of the drugs. As I sat in front of a nurses' station in a wheelchair, I noticed several patients staring at me. It was quite frightening. My mom stayed with me the whole time, comforting me.

Then I met Dr. Francis Cancellieri, the psychiatrist in charge on the floor. He began to ask me questions, which I could not even answer. I was completely numb at this point. They put me in a room, and I remember crying inconsolably until I fell asleep.

During that night, I was at one point on the phone with my husband, and I was begging him to come and have me discharged. A very kind person came into the room by the payphone and found me with my hands over my face, crying my eyes out. Her name was Audrey Stephanski. She tried to comfort me and spoke so softly. I felt immediate comfort. When I looked up, I realized that I knew her. Her son Matt and I were friends all through school, and she knew my family well. About ten years before that, Matt had died from a gunshot to the mouth. She sat with me and shared some very personal stories. Audrey believed Matt had been murdered. These stories helped take my mind off my troubles.

I thought it was the hand of the Lord that night. Maybe He was trying to show me something. Maybe there were bigger things to think about besides myself and my self-pity. I was so scared in that hospital. When I left that room, I got some sleep that night after a big hug from Audrey.

The next morning, I met some of the regular nurses on the floor, who were very nice to me. They had a soft side and knew exactly how to deal with someone feeling as low as I felt. Some of the other patients joined me in the recreation room. Everyone seemed as normal as I thought I was. Most of them had major depression or drug addictions. Some were suicidal or had bipolar disorder.

My diagnosis was post-traumatic stress disorder (PTSD) and major depression. I met some people who mostly stayed in bed and asked for medication every four hours. I caught on to that quickly, so I began to do the same. Then I could just sleep this nightmare away. The staff kept me on heavy Valium and antidepressants around the clock.

That second day, I felt so lost. I thought I had finally cracked and would never be normal again. Good grief, I was on a psychiatric floor. That gave me a sickening feeling. I thought my mental state would never recover. I was officially a crackpot. I desperately did not want anyone to find out. I nearly died when I found out the hospital would notify my job of my admission. Workplaces have to maintain confidentiality, but let's be realistic: word travels fast.

Within a week, the flight attendant grapevine got wind of the real reasons for my absence. Before I knew it, I had two hundred get-well cards from flight attendants. That number is not an exaggeration. Everyone was very supportive, thankfully.

FATE AND DR. CANCELLIERI

Dr. Cancellieri turned out to be a wonderful doctor. Coincidentally, he had once worked with the FBI's antiterrorist task force. In fact, he knew the agents who had interviewed me on 9/11. I felt very comfortable with Dr. Cancellieri, and I began my therapy sessions in the hospital with him.

On my second day, my husband brought my children to visit me, which I was not happy about. I did not want them to see me like this. They were not prepared for this type of place. My two little ones were completely freaked out by the unfamiliar surroundings.

When my family was ready to leave, I tried to leave with them. I sneaked past the nurses' station, but a security guard escorted me off the elevator. I was hysterical because my family was leaving me there again. I did not think I could handle another night. I felt so alone and vulnerable. They left anyway.

Because I had tried to sneak out of there, I lost my privileges for smoking. The nurses took patients outside several times a day for a cigarette. That seemed to be the only pleasure of the day, those short walks downstairs. I had thrown away the only ounce of enjoyment I had in that place.

I insisted the staff call the doctor to sign me out of there. I waited for Dr. Cancellieri. He did sign me out but highly recommended I stay for at least three days for evaluation. I left the hospital AMA (against medical advice). I did promise Dr. Cancellieri, however, that I would call his office the next day and see him as an outpatient, and so I did.

I became very comfortable with Dr. Cancellieri. I felt as if he understood me as a person. He made me feel quite normal, not like a crazy or confused person. He often stressed to me the effects of post-traumatic stress disorder, reminding me that what I was experiencing was normal. I finally have come to terms with that diagnosis. The PTSD is the reason, I guess, that I am having so much trouble getting past 9/11.

DR. KILROY

While Dr. Cancellieri monitored my medications, I also saw a psychologist, Dr. James Kilroy. I found him through a church friend. I chose him because he was a Christian psychologist, and I had a strong belief in my Recovery Bible (an edition of the Bible with the twelve steps of addiction recovery in it) and healing through the Lord. At that period of my life and in my depression, the only relief I found was in my scriptures.

Dr. Kilroy was outstanding in therapy. We touched on so many issues that I needed to deal with in my life. I felt like I was carrying a sunken chest full of dead weight inside. He taught me that when the trauma hit me, every other unresolved issue in my life surfaced, and everything felt ten times worse.

I had never felt so completely hopeless as I did after the attacks. I lay on my couch for about six months, avoiding contact with any- and everyone. My kids came home from school every day and found me not showered and still in pajamas, usually crying or reading my Bible. It is the only thing I did for many months. It was a very dark and desperate time for me. I did not know how to crawl out.

This led to the most important loss I experienced from 9/11. That loss was the separation from my youngest child, Donnie. Because I could not function enough to take care of him, in March 2002, he went to live with his dad in South Jersey.

During this time, I had no interest whatsoever in seeing anyone. I canceled so many appointments with Dr. Kilroy that he finally dropped me as a patient. How do you get dropped by a psychologist? Messing with his schedule is how I seemed to do it!

RETURNING TO WORK, MAY 2002

The time at home after the hospital visit in January was very difficult. I returned to work in May because I thought I had dealt with the trauma and gotten all the help that I needed. I felt well and ready to dive into the work that I loved so much. I had therapy and doctors and medication.

I cried and talked to the doctors about my fears and my yearning to console the flight attendants. For some strange reason, I felt that they needed me. Not just any coordinator—it was me I thought they needed. When I look back on those distorted thoughts, perhaps I needed the flight attendants to need me. It was all for my gratification. I was not willing to admit that I was still in emotional overload, a wreck. I couldn't even tell myself that I was. I believed I was as good as new and probably better since I had been to counseling.

The doctors sent me back to work in May 2002 with antidepressants and Xanax for anxiety. My care team had advised me to take medication while at work to ease the anxiety and get through the hard times. I thought I was so strong at that point, but I couldn't have been more wrong. The guilt I carried over those women who went on Flight 93 ate away at me. My self-care hit a new low as I became sicker by the day.

Eventually, my guilt and depression led to drug addiction in 2005.

EMOTIONAL BREAKDOWN

Over the years, the people I have spoken to about clinical depression or post-traumatic stress disorder do not fully understand the seriousness of these diagnoses. Many do not realize the impact these conditions can have on one's life or one's family. My experiences with these illnesses have changed my life.

People seem to think that you can "shake it" and just move on. The Lord knows that I have tried everything possible to overcome this battle. In my experience so far, it has been virtually impossible without therapy and medication combined. Sometimes my confused brain fills with loneliness, and I can't quite stay with one thought long enough to concentrate. I still try to maintain my moods and stay aware of them; it is a daily struggle.

Now, in 2006, I search for spiritual growth. It has taken me a long time to recognize its importance in my life. Deep prayer works best for me. This involves sitting quietly for long periods of time, meditating, listening, quieting the mind, and talking to God. I have also found that it hurts me emotionally to stay bitter toward people who have been unkind to me. Forgiveness is necessary.

For a time, I turned to drugs to numb the pain. At the time I started down that path, I never would have believed that. I thought I just wanted to party. But now, looking back, I think it all began as a part of my trauma. From about 2005 to 2015, I went down a road of self-destruction on drugs, trying to forget myself and my misery. It didn't work. It just destroyed my family and me for a long time; broken hearts, broken promises, and disappointments took their toll.

My children finally intervened when I found myself in Butler, Pennsylvania, with a brain aneurysm. After I had had several ministrokes, my son and daughter-in-law, Jason and Leanne, brought me back to New Jersey to mend and get my life back.

Today I participate in a twelve-step program, and I feel clean and serene and live my best life possible. I am so grateful for my children and my family. I am truly blessed.

Another tip I learned from Dr. Kilroy, my psychologist, is to listen to my body. If it says it is tired, then I listen and give it an emotional rest. I clear my head, take a bath, or take a mental-health walk. This has turned into some of the most important advice I have received.

I already know that I can no longer handle the things in life that I used to. I probably never will, but at least I know how to care for Terry—myself—healthily. I also have learned that God wants us to realize how precious we are to Him and to see ourselves in the light of His love. If God considered us worth giving up the most precious thing He had (His Son), what does that say about how valuable we are to Him (see Psalm 8, King James Bible)?

I have also learned that I no longer have to justify my illness or my behavior to anyone except the good Lord above. I must say that nothing ticks me off more than someone advising me to "move on and get over it." As the stressors in my life come upon me, I must learn to handle them like an adult, a sane and emotionally sound adult. I am not the most stable adult yet, but I will work on that until I am.

The Lord has a record of all my wrongs, and He has forgiven me and washed my soul clean. I have unloaded a lot of the guilt that has weighed me down, and I continue to learn to make peace with that. I worked through a Recovery Bible for a long time while I sat confused on the beaches in Pensacola, Florida. Looking at myself in complete honesty is critical. We need to be honest about our past hurts, express our feelings, confront the guilt, and work through forgiveness. If we try to ignore these hurts, our explosive, hidden emotions will control us. This idea comes from my Recovery Bible and reflects the denial in my own life.

At many moments, I have thought, "This is it. I can never recover or never fix this mess in my life." Every time, no matter what the circumstance, the Lord steps in and reminds me that He always remains with me. I start my scripture reading and church-going again.

While I struggle to stay disciplined with my Bible, I need it to live a healthy, peaceful life. Putting all my cares into the hands of God works every time. I find such comfort in that. He will let me stray only so far off track from His plan for me, and He always pulls me back into His loving care. Praise God. "Commit thy way unto the Lord; trust also in him; and he shall bring it to pass" (Psalms 37:5 KJV).

Anyone suffering from depression must accept that he or she has a lifelong illness. It, along with post-traumatic stress disorder, requires a delicate and timely touch. My trauma from 9/11 has still not fully revealed itself, nor have I healed from it. Other traumas and stressors in my life since then have led me off the course of recovery. I can give a lot of advice to women by saying that despite the bumps and loneliness of that road, you must find your path through and feel the pain. Then comfort will come—and closure, eventually. Then you can experience some kind of healing. The emotions I have experienced seem so strange to me and quite hard to describe, even to my doctors.

I sometimes feel as if I have many sides to my personality—not anything like schizophrenia or psychosis, thank God! I have never had delusions or any of the more serious mental symptoms. I have, however, become extremely violent while self-medicating with alcohol and drugs. At times, I would not back down from anyone, even a man. Many confrontations happened with the men in my life. I now can look at myself honestly and take responsibility for my shortcomings and work through them in therapy and with my higher power.

PRIORITIES HAVE CHANGED

My children and God are what matter to me. The guilt I carry from my mom's death will take a long time to resolve, but I will continue to confront my feelings and grief. I will share some of the most shaming decisions that I have made and the pain they caused those dear to me. I hope that these stories will benefit someone who is confused or suffers from these symptoms. For your own sake, seek professional help.

Almost every hospital offers a mental-health doctor or clinic. It could be a matter of life and death, as it became for me in 2005. In 2002 and 2003, when I thought I was at my lowest, I felt quite embarrassed to tell anyone that I had major depression and post-traumatic stress disorder. I didn't understand them completely. Thanks to the doctors and much therapy and medication, I now understand the human psyche and how trauma affects it.

If the issue becomes drugs or alcohol, then I highly recommend a twelve-step program, as it is doing wonders for me. It changes my life daily. It has taught me to love myself and no longer harm myself.

Dr. Kilroy, my psychologist, explained to me that we have patterns—often dysfunctional ones—in our lives and personalities. He helped me to realize that these patterns do not change until we figure out where they began. Where did we learn these behaviors?

I have worked intensely on that question since 9/11. In my case, I put so much pressure on myself to bounce back from 9/11 that I failed to realize that my problems run so much deeper. I have taken a good look at my childhood and my family traits, just trying to figure out what is wrong with me. Why can't I shake this mess in my head? I found that in therapy, I had to deal with that stuff you see on posters in the psychiatric offices: the inner child. It turns out that the way you felt as a child often affects how you behave and handle things as an adult. My inner child needs a lot of healing from the pain and longing for my father.

I have had many dysfunctional men in my life, and I catered to them. Now I have learned so much and worked so much on myself that I can look back on my decisions and recognize that pattern. I longed so badly for the unconditional love of my dad that I would have taken it from anyone.

My father, whom I loved so dearly despite his problems, suffered for many years and died on April 6, 2006, with his primary killer being his liver because of self-destruction. During my life, I had looked at him as my hero. I always blamed Mom for his troubles. Dad had alcohol- and drug-addiction issues. He also spent quite some time in jail. Thankfully, he came out of prison drug free. He continued to drink, however.

I remember so many times visiting him while he was in prison. My mom, my brother, and I would stand in line while the guards checked our bags and our sub sandwiches. Then we would wait with all the other families for the prisoners to come into a big room with a bunch of round tables in it. The other couples practically had sex right there. When Dad finally came into the room, I would cry uncontrollably for the whole visit. It was such a traumatic time for me as a child.

Dad did woodworking while he was in prison. He made airplanes for my brother, Steve, including a beautiful Red Baron aircraft. Dad made jewelry boxes lined with velvet for me. I wish that I had treasured them and kept them forever. Dad wrote me hundreds of letters and found the Lord in jail. When he came out, he tried so hard to live a normal life, but I guess he had hereditary alcoholism. Regardless, my dad died as my hero, and I still felt like his little girl. I took his death hard.

Grandma's death devastated the whole family. She was the core of the family. She and Pop had three daughters: Linda, Kathy (my mother), and Laurie. The daughters together had a total of seven children. Everything went on at Grandma's house, and she talked to each of her daughters daily, so we all always knew what each other were up to. I was very close to Grandma. She died on November 30, 1999.

I, along with the rest of the family, spent the last week with her in the hospice ward of Riverview Hospital in Red Bank, New Jersey. We spent so much time together when I was a child, and when I became a mother myself, Grandma was my everything. She had a great way with the grandkids. Everyone loved Gram Bernice. My grandfather Bill is still with us today and will turn eighty-nine on December 3, 2006.

After spending every possible moment with my grandmother in the hospital for six days, I finally went in to work a shift at the airport. Oddly, during one of my busiest times at work (the London flight's check-in), I had a strong urge to call the hospital. My aunt Linda got on the phone and said that Grandma was just taking her last breaths. I felt special because she had "waited" for me. Grandma lived a loving and full life, and I felt she was at peace now. But that didn't make it any easier for any of us.

MOM'S ILLNESS

In the spring of 2004, my mom was tested for a spot they found on her lung. The doctors decided to have the growth removed to be safe.

On the day of the surgery, Anne (Mom's best friend) and I went with her to the hospital. Mom felt understandably nervous. The surgery was supposed to be a couple of hours, but it took three hours longer than planned. Most of the family was at the hospital, waiting for word from the doctors. It was so scary when hour by hour went by with no word.

Finally, when the doctor came out, he said Mom had lesions behind the rib cage and would have to have aggressive chemotherapy right away. I thought I would die. Anne was devastated by the news. We all stayed strong for Mom's sake.

Within weeks, Mom started her cancer treatments and very quickly began to lose her hair and have awful side effects. I went to her house every morning following the surgery because she needed to stay in bed to heal. I helped the best I could with the house and with taking care of Mom. I felt so good being able to help her. Just being able to be there for her was so fulfilling to me. I never once thought that this was the beginning to the end of Mom's life. But it was.

Mom began to get depressed with the side effects, and the sickness was taking a toll on her. I bought her a couple of books on chemotherapy and cancer so she could know what to expect. It was all very surreal. We never for a moment thought that this illness would take her at such a young age.

Anne and I took Mom to a wig store once she was ready to wear a wig. For a while, she wouldn't even leave the house while her hair was falling out. She did find a wig, however, and looked great in it. It was summer, though, so she was hot and uncomfortable.

Mom had a very strong faith in God and a belief in her healing. She never stopped fighting, and everyone around her could see that. I never once heard her complain, even at the worst point of the disease. Mom went into remission in the fall.

My mother, Kathy McGowan, married my stepfather, Joe, when my brother, Steve, and I were teenagers. She had another child, Meghan, when I was eighteen years old. Mom also went to nursing school during my junior-high years. She was so driven to do better. She was a real worker, having been waitressing six nights a week at the same place for over eighteen years. She busted her tail for my brother and me when we were young.

Mom was a real role model and an incredible influence on my kids. She was the perfect grandmother to them. She couldn't have possibly shown them more love than she did, and she treated them like her own. She never missed a birthday party or any kind of party celebrating my kids. She adored them, and it showed every day. My children went to my mother for everything.

She has walked me through some of the most trying times in my life. She never turned me away and was such an encouraging, positive cheerleader for me throughout my life.

A few months after Mom's remission, cancer returned. This time the doctors saw it on the liver and lower section of the lung. I know now that it was inevitable that it would kill her, but at the time, I refused to believe how bad it was. Shortly after that news, I began drinking heavily again. I think it was an escape for me. The drinking made life so much easier to live.

In February 2005, Mom and Anne came over to do a kind of intervention with me. Mom accused me of drinking too much and tried to get me to go to the hospital. She even called my psychiatrist,

Dr. Cancellieri. I was so mad about that, but she did it out of love. When I wouldn't listen to Mom, she had my three older kids come stay at her house (Donnie was living in South Jersey with his dad). This devastated me. I felt like such a failure but wouldn't give in. I was busy being selfish with my partying.

Mom threatened several times to call child services because of my behavior. But I never listened. I knew the kids were okay with her, but I didn't realize how sick she was or I was.

I ran away to Florida with a man I hardly knew and stayed away for more than a year. What kind of mother does that? What kind of daughter does that? My mother did call child services, and they gave the care of the children to my mom. She again was saving me for the sake of those beautiful kids of mine.

I was on drugs with that man, and I couldn't stop using. The addiction had set in. Could it all have started with my trauma? I will never know. I do know that it progressed for about ten years until I sought help.

Mom died on November 28, 2005, while I was in a psychiatric hospital in North Carolina. She was fifty-nine years old.

DEATH AND DESPAIR

The forty-one-year-old man that I loved died very suddenly in March 2005 from a heart problem. In November 2005, my mother died of cancer. In April 2006, I lost my sixty-one-year-old father because of many illnesses that poisoned his body. In November 2006, I lost my granddaughter Hannah Michelle, who only lived for five minutes after being born prematurely. Witnessing the pain that my daughter and my son-in-law endured when that beautiful child passed was one of the hardest times in my life. Nothing can compare with the agony that you feel for your child when they hurt.

When I reflect on the devastating circumstances my family and I have endured in such a short period, it makes me so sad. I began to look elsewhere for comfort, and that brought me to a long, lonely road of drug addiction in 2005.

As the doctor explains it, I have not had time to deal with my post-traumatic stress from 9/11. The other circumstances thrown at me have been too overwhelming to face. I have learned that you must open each door of that pain and feel that pain again to heal from it. You must face those demons, so to speak, and slowly work through them.

I think that is one of my biggest issues. I am afraid to face them. I very rarely think about my parents, and I know why. This is something I would like to talk about with the psychiatrist, something I need to talk about and work through. I know I am denying and burying those painful feelings. I do not want to feel them, and I cannot quite bring myself there to this day. I tell myself that the Lord is guiding me through all the hurts when He sees I am ready to work through them and heal. Finding myself incapable of grieving completely leaves me feeling very guilty.

I feel sure that my mother and father are a part of my life and watching me, so that comfort I feel from them is enough for now. Their deaths were such a huge loss to me that I feel that my mind is once again protecting me. The human psyche is quite amazing; perhaps my mind is shielding me from the pain thrown at me all at once. I seem to take it in small doses and work very hard to find comfort in the end. I make a conscious effort not to think about my parents in my everyday life.

I am so afraid to feel those emotions that come with the thought of my parents. It starts with a thought of them; then the thought process brings me to a feeling and then the emotions. I learned in the hospital that the thought can change as soon as you have it to avoid that feeling. It starts with a thought. It is a very simple process that most people cope with many times throughout life, but I feel far from being like other people. I feel very ill without medication and doctors' care. I am scared to death to be without either one. I am confident that the emotions will come in small doses so I can feel the pain and appreciate my loved ones for who they were when they were alive.

I have been working on accepting my parents' deaths at such young ages. A great tip I got was from someone in a grief-counseling group in a church in Virginia. This person told me to set up a photo of my parents, Fred (my deceased boyfriend), my grandbaby, my grandmother, or my flight attendants, then light a candle and spend time talking to those deceased loved ones. I have found that when I have done that with my parents' photo, the overwhelming emotions and uncontrollable crying came along with that. It was so empowering because I felt I allowed myself to feel those feelings and speak to my parents. I also felt their presence. It was a very comforting place to be.

CONCLUSION

Wow, it is already March 2008. I haven't picked up my story in my journal in about six months. It seems to be the way I have written over the past five or six years. I find myself in a funk all the time. It's getting quite old, though.

I have been through other relationships with a few jerks. Thank God that, through therapy and my growing process and maturing, I have learned to value myself and learn what is normal in a loving relationship. I have found that I deserve a good man in my life. I can now look back with disgust and wonder where on Earth my head was when I got caught up and involved with such scum at times. I deserve the best, and I will no longer settle for less.

I continue to struggle with the six medications that my psychiatrist has prescribed for me. I hate taking them and often do not do it. When I do, I stay focused and balanced—that is, I do when I stay walking with God *and* taking my meds. I find that if I just do my own thing and try to stay numb to my problems and my current situation, I stay in that funk, and my life goes nowhere.

That has been my problem. I look back, and I feel that I have lost the last five years completely. The time has just passed, and I have pretty much wasted it. I have to get my head out of the sand and put my life back on track. "This is the year Terry will be back to herself," I keep telling myself. I intend on accomplishing that, and I pray for the strength and discipline to carry on.

Since I have written last, I have endured the deaths of my uncle Reed and my grandfather. Both were such strong and wonderful roles in my life, real men in my eyes. They were probably the only men to be positive influences on me while I was growing up. They both always showed love and genuine concern for me. Either one would have done anything for me.

Well, I cannot forget my brother, so I take that back. Steve Horniacek is the man in my life whom I most admire and am incredibly proud to know. He is the most outstanding father, husband, and brother. Steve is very successful with his business in Pennsylvania, and the community respects him. He has built a beautiful life for his wife and five children. It's amazing. I am such a mess all the time, and I have a brother whose shoes anyone would kill to be in. He has worked hard for his life and deserves to reap the benefits and blessings. I am so proud to be his sister that there are not even words to describe how I feel about him. I can count on Steve for anything, always.

Back in May 2007, my grandfather Bill Petrasek died. It was very difficult, as Pop was a father to me.

The date is now April 14, 2010. It has been that long since I have had the courage and the motivation to continue writing. Although this terror from 9/11/01 has not been minimized in my thoughts, I have learned over the years to recognize the triggers of the stress and trauma. I have had many years of therapy at this point, and I thank God for that. The ten or so doctors I have seen and had treatment with have all given me the same diagnosis of major depressive disorder and post-traumatic stress disorder. For a few years, they said I was bipolar, but then the workers' compensation doctor disagreed with that diagnosis. Nonetheless, the moods I live with are extreme.

When I behave erratically, it is not obvious to me at the time. But when the behavior ends, I can sit back and reflect; then I realize how crazy and how frightening these moods are. I spiral into and out of depression all these years later. September 11 was nine years ago, so I assume this will never go away.

Today, I am still in therapy, but it is only every two weeks, I am happy to say, and I have a great relationship with my therapist,

Shelby. She has gotten me through a lot of hard times over the past couple of years. I am also still on medications for my depression, as I imagine I will always need them, but I am okay with that.

The most rewarding thing is that today I am clean and happy, and I have complete and total serenity from my drug addiction. I still suffer from PTSD, but it gets easier year after year. This year, I am trying to muster up the courage to attend the 2021 memorial at the Shanksville crash site with my sponsor.

God bless the crew of United Flight 93, and God bless America.

ABOUT THE AUTHOR

Theresa Ann Horniacek was born and raised in a small town on the Jersey Shore called Highlands. After graduating from high school, she attended the Wilma Boyd Trade School. From there, she landed a job at Newark International Airport as a customer-service agent.

During that time, Theresa got married and had four children. She also worked at a Head Start program, where she ran the parents' volunteer program and implemented literacy-training, job-readiness, and GED-training classes. Theresa received a humanitarian award for her difference-making work in this program.

Afterward, Theresa landed a great job at United Airlines as an in-flight-services coordinator. Her duties included briefing crews, following FAA guidelines, and keeping the Chicago crew desk updated. During United Airlines' Health Awareness Month, she set up and implemented a mammogram program. For these efforts, the

CEO of United presented Mrs. Horniacek with another humanitarian award.

Within six months of this success, 9/11 occurred, as detailed in this book. Theresa's trauma in the 9/11 experience brought her to a dark place of PTSD, severe depression and anxiety, and crippling drug addiction.

Horniacek put herself into intense trauma therapy with Dr. Cancellieri and learned how to start living again. Placed on medications for her diagnoses, Theresa overcame the odds thanks to intervention by her family that led to her reentering life and reacquainting herself with God. She is now thriving in a twelve-step program, in which she continues to recover working with her sponsor, sponsoring other women, and fulfilling speaking commitments. Every week, Theresa participates in therapy through an intensive outpatient program (IOP). Her therapist guides her through a Seeking Safety program, which has taught her the skills to cope with daily triggers and recurring nightmares.

Most mornings, Theresa enjoys reading her Bible, writing, and working on her IOP. She faithfully takes direction for her care from her doctors. Theresa's inspiration for this book was to help people like her to function better in life and achieve goals beyond their limitations. She says, "If I can, you can!"

CPSIA information can be obtained
at www.ICGtesting.com
Printed in the USA
LVHW080734270522
719905LV00002B/41